A MORBID TASTE FOR BONES

Detectives come in all shapes and sizes, in any place and in any century. Today there is Inspector Morse; last century there was Sherlock Holmes; and eight centuries ago, in the great abbey at Shrewsbury, there was Brother Cadfael.

Brother Cadfael is a monk. He is the abbey's gardener and knows a great deal about plants and herbs, and their medicinal uses. He also understands people, which is very useful when Prior Robert decides to go to Wales to bring back the bones of a long-dead saint. In the twelfth century every great church and abbey wants to have some holy relics, and Prior Robert believes it is God's wish that the bones of Saint Winifred should come to Shrewsbury.

But the people of Gwytherin in the Welsh hills don't see it like that at all. Why should their very own Saint Winifred be taken away to England, a foreign country? And when murder is done, it will need all Brother Cadfael's experience and understanding to find the murderer. In fact, it will need a miracle . . .

OXFORD BOOKWORMS LIBRARY

Crime & Mystery

A Morbid Taste for Bones

Stage 4 (1400 headwords)

Series Editor: Jennifer Bassett
Founder Editor: Tricia Hedge
Activities Editors: Jennifer Bassett and Christine Lindop

ELLIS PETERS

A Morbid Taste
for Bones

Retold by
John Escott

Illustrated by
Axel Rator

OXFORD UNIVERSITY PRESS

OXFORD
UNIVERSITY PRESS

Great Clarendon Street, Oxford OX2 6DP

Oxford New York

Auckland Bangkok Buenos Aires Cape Town Chennai
Dar es Salaam Delhi Hong Kong Istanbul Karachi Kolkata
Kuala Lumpur Madrid Melbourne Mexico City Mumbai Nairobi
São Paulo Shanghai Singapore Taipei Tokyo Toronto
and an associated company in Berlin

OXFORD and OXFORD ENGLISH are registered trade marks
of Oxford University Press in the UK and in certain other countries

ISBN 0 19 423040 6

Original edition copyright © Ellis Peters 1977
First published by Macmillan London Limited 1977
This simplified edition © Oxford University Press 2002
First published in the Oxford Bookworms Library 2002

Database right Oxford University Press (maker)

Printed in Spain by Unigraf s.l.

CONTENTS

PEOPLE IN THIS STORY

1

Saint Winifred's story

It was a fine, bright morning in early May, and Brother Cadfael was working in the garden of Shrewsbury Abbey. It was peaceful there, and he enjoyed the work. He grew the vegetables for the abbey kitchens, and the herbs which were used for cooking or for making medicines.

'There's no better Benedictine garden in the whole country,' he thought, proudly. He had planted many unusual herbs during his fifteen years at the abbey – herbs collected during his travels in Venice, Cyprus, and the Holy Land, before he had come to Shrewsbury. As a young man he had had an interesting and varied life. 'See that brother working in the garden?' the other monks whispered to each other when he first came. 'He used to be a sea captain, working for the King of Jerusalem, all along the coast of the Holy Land!'

Brother Cadfael saw nothing strange about this. He had enjoyed his adventures at sea, and now in his fifties he was enjoying the peace and quiet of a monk's life.

He looked across the garden at his two helpers, Brother John and Brother Columbanus. They were working near the tall poppies, whose purple flowers could make strong medicines to take away pain, or to help a man sleep. Cadfael watched the two young men stand up, and brush their dirty hands against the rough material of their habits.

1

'It must be time for morning prayers,' thought Cadfael. 'Brother Columbanus doesn't like to be late.'

Brother Columbanus, a tall, strong, young man, with yellow hair and blue eyes, was always trying to be the perfect monk. The younger son of an important family, he expected

Brother Cadfael looked across the garden at his two helpers.

to rise to the very top in his monastic life. He was alarmingly enthusiastic about his work and prayers, and often had strange dreams and visions. Sometimes his excitement was so extreme that he fell down in a fit, lying unconscious for hours. The poppy medicine had often helped to calm him.

'But he's young,' Brother Cadfael thought. 'And I've every hope that he has time to get over his problems.'

Brother John was not the kind of monk to have visions. A square young man, with a circle of red-brown hair, he was sensible, kind, and able to see the funny side of life. Cadfael thought he was not really suited to the quiet life of the abbey, and wondered if he would stay. Meanwhile, Brother John enjoyed life when he could.

'I mustn't be late,' he said now, smiling happily. 'I'm reader this week.'

'You read for the glory of God and the saints, brother,' said Columbanus, 'not for your own!'

*   *   *

The morning prayers did not take long, and afterwards the monks followed Abbot Heribert into the meeting-house, for the usual daily discussions of abbey business.

Abbot Heribert was a gentle old man, who never spoke in anger. Behind him came Prior Robert, a much more alarming figure. He was tall and thin, with silver-grey hair, and when he spoke, people listened. Although still only a prior at the moment, he planned to become an abbot one day, and he had no doubts that he would succeed.

Cadfael found his seat in the meeting-house. He often went

to sleep in his dark corner. This morning he stayed awake long enough to hear Brother John read, then shut his eyes and made himself comfortable. 'Prior Robert is going to talk about finding the relics of a saint for the monastery,' he thought. 'He's been talking about it for a year now. I really can't listen to all that again!' And he was soon asleep.

Cadfael was quite right. Prior Robert was desperate to find a really good saint. Another abbey, not that far away, had recently brought the bones of a famous saint to their church, and were very proud of this. And here – as Prior Robert said so often – was the great Benedictine abbey of Shrewsbury without a single relic to its name!

Cadfael slept peacefully through the report of the prior's searches, and then was suddenly woken by a loud scream.

Brother Columbanus was on the ground, beating his head and hands on the stone floor. Cadfael and two other monks ran and knelt beside him to stop him breaking his bones or cutting his head open.

'A fit!' said one of the monks.

'Poor young man!' said the abbot. 'Take him to the sick rooms and put him to bed. We must pray for him.'

They got Columbanus into a bed and Cadfael gave him some poppy medicine to calm him.

'Someone must watch him,' said Prior Robert. 'Brother Jerome, you will stay with him.'

'Oh, I'll be pleased to!' said Brother Jerome. He followed the prior like a dog, and was always happy to obey his orders. The prior knew this and was not slow to make use of Jerome.

'He'll sleep soon,' said Cadfael. 'With God's help, he'll be better in the morning.'

* * *

The next day, when Brother Jerome arrived at the meeting-house, he was very excited.

'Is our brother better?' the abbot asked him.

'He's sleeping at the moment, but not peacefully,' said Jerome. 'And when he wakes, he is confused and talks wildly, like a madman. But, Father, in the night I had a dream!'

'Then let us hear it,' said the abbot.

'Father, the wall of the room seemed to open and a great light shone in,' said Jerome. 'And a beautiful young woman came and stood by Brother Columbanus' bed, and spoke to me. "My name is Winifred," she said. "In Wales there is a holy well at the place where I died. If Brother Columbanus washes in the water from the well, he will get better." Then she disappeared in a great light, and I woke up!'

'Father Abbot!' cried Prior Robert. 'It is a sign! This saint knows about our search, and is calling to us!'

'Winifred?' said the abbot. 'I don't remember the story of this saint. There are so many of them in Wales. But certainly, Brother Columbanus must go to her holy well. We must not seem ungrateful for this sign. But where exactly is the well?'

There were several Welshmen, as well as Cadfael, among the brothers. The prior looked quickly past Cadfael, who was not one of his favourites. 'Brother Rhys,' he said. 'Can you tell us about this saint, and where we can find her holy well?'

Brother Rhys was old and toothless, and usually forgotten.

He stared, surprised, at the ring of faces looking at him now. 'Saint Winifred's well?' he said. 'You'll find it in Holywell, not far from Chester. But you won't find her grave there.'

'Tell us her story,' said Prior Robert.

'Saint Winifred,' said the old man, beginning to enjoy himself, 'was the only child of a man called Tevyth. When Saint Beuno came to that part of Wales, Tevyth and his family became his followers. The saint lived with Tevyth and his family, and they built him a church nearby. Winifred loved God and said her prayers every day, but one Sunday she was ill and did not go to church, so her parents left her alone in the house. Now, at that time the king had a son called Cradoc, and this prince was secretly in love with Winifred, who was very beautiful. That morning, he came to her house, saying he had been riding and was very thirsty. Winifred invited him inside for a drink of water. Then he jumped on her, threw his arms round her, and pushed her to the floor.

'Winifred fought him off, and escaping to another room, climbed out of a window. She ran to the church, but Cradoc jumped on his horse and rode after her. He caught her just before she got to the church, and fearing that she would tell everyone about him and what he had done, he cut off her head with his sword!

'But people were already coming out of the church, and they all saw him kill her. Saint Beuno immediately put a curse on Cradoc, and he disappeared into the ground. Then Saint Beuno put Winifred's head onto her neck – and she stood up, alive again! And the holy well appeared in that very place.'

'And afterwards?' asked Prior Robert. 'What did Saint Winifred do with the rest of her life?'

'She went to Rome to meet other saints,' said Brother Rhys. 'Then she came back to Wales and went to live at Gwytherin. She lived many years, and did many miracles.'

'Is her grave at Gwytherin?' asked the prior. 'And did the miracles continue after her death?'

'That's what I've heard,' said the old man. 'But it's a long time since I heard anyone talk about her.'

Prior Robert turned to look at Abbot Heribert. 'Father, this gentle saint came to us in Brother Jerome's dream. If she answers our prayers and makes Brother Columbanus well again, will the church agree to let us bring her relics here, to Shrewsbury, to the great glory of our house?'

'And to the glory of Prior Robert,' whispered Brother John in Cadfael's ear.

'Well, she certainly seems to be giving us a sign,' said Abbot Heribert.

'So may I send Brother Columbanus and Brother Jerome to Holywell this very day?' asked the prior.

'Yes, with the prayers of us all,' said the abbot.

* * *

The two brothers were gone for five days, and when they came home, Brother Columbanus' face was bright and clear. He went straight to the church to give prayers of thanks to God and Saint Winifred, then he and Jerome went to report to the abbot, the prior and the sub-prior.

'Father,' said Brother Columbanus, 'I came out of my

terrible dream to find a bright morning and a world of spring. I was standing without my clothes, in the grass beside a well, and Brother Jerome was putting water over me. "Where am I?" I asked. "Why am I here?" And he told me. Saint Winifred has saved me, Father, and I thank her with all my heart.'

Brother Jerome spoke next. In a voice full of wonder, he described how Columbanus lost his madness at the first touch of the holy water. 'And Father,' he went on, 'the village people say that the saint is indeed buried at Gwytherin, and that many miracles have happened there. But they also say that nobody takes care of her grave any more.'

'Saint Winifred is calling us to save her from that place!' cried Prior Robert. 'There can be no mistake! Father Abbot, let me bring this holy lady to rest here among us, and to bring us glory!'

'In the name of God, yes,' said Abbot Heribert.

*   *   *

'It was all planned,' said Brother John, in the herb garden later. 'The prior knew about Saint Winifred all the time.'

'And Brother Columbanus' falling fit?' said Cadfael, smiling. 'Was that planned, too?'

Brother John thought seriously for a moment. 'No, but we all know our brother gets over-excited and often has fits. To throw ice-cold water over him is one good way to bring him out of it – but he didn't have to go all the way to Holywell for that! However, *he'll* believe what they tell him, and agree that Saint Winifred saved him. Remember, the prior told *Jerome* to stay with Columbanus that night. It takes only one man to

*'Father Abbot,' cried Prior Robert, 'let me bring this holy lady
to rest here among us, and to bring us glory!'*

have a vision, but it has to be the right man. And it will be the right men who go to Wales with Prior Robert – and that won't be us, Brother Cadfael!'

No doubt about it, this young man wanted to breathe the air and look at the world outside the abbey walls once again. Cadfael also found the idea pleasing. Perhaps, he thought, there was a way for them both to go.

He went to see the abbot. 'I think it is important for somebody to go who is able to speak Welsh,' he said. 'The priest and people of Gwytherin will probably not speak much English, if any.'

'True,' agreed the abbot. 'Brother Cadfael, Welsh is your first language. Will you go with them?'

'Of course, Father,' said Cadfael, smiling to himself. 'But there is a young brother here with us, and I'm worried about him. I'm not sure he is suited to a monk's life. Will you let me take him with me? It will give him time to think, and he can cut wood and fetch water for us.'

Abbot Heribert looked a little worried. 'Have you, er, talked to Prior Robert about this young man?' he asked.

'Prior Robert,' replied Cadfael, keeping his face very serious, 'has so many more important things to think about. I didn't like to trouble him . . .'

'Quite right!' said the abbot, thankfully. 'Prior Robert can be . . . well, rather hard on those who have doubts. All right. Tell me this brother's name, and he can go with you.'

2

A MEETING IN THE WOODS

P rior Robert was not pleased when he heard that Brother Cadfael and Brother John were coming to Wales with him, but the abbot had spoken, so there was nothing the prior could do about it. Brother Jerome was going, of course, and Brother Columbanus. The sixth monk in the party was Brother Richard, the sub-prior, a clever but lazy man, who liked a quiet life.

They began their journey as soon as the reliquary for the saint's bones was ready, a fine coffin made of dark wood and bright silver. First, they went to Bangor, to get agreement for their plan from the church and the king. Bishop David gave the plan his blessing, and Prince Owain, who spoke for his father the king, also agreed – and helpfully sent one of his men, Urien, to show them the best way to Gwytherin.

So, in the third week of May, leaving the coast, they rode up into the Welsh hills, and came at last to a high valley, with thick forests and green fields running down each side of a river. As they rode down into the Gwytherin valley, they saw a small stone church and a little wooden house beside it.

'There's the church and the priest's house,' said Urien. 'We'll go there first, and I'll introduce you to Father Huw.'

As they arrived, a small, square man with brown hair, a beard, and dark-blue eyes came out of the house.

'Good-day, Father Huw,' said Urien. 'I've brought you important visitors on church business, and with the blessing of prince and bishop.' He introduced them all by name. 'And have no fear when I have gone, for Brother Cadfael here speaks Welsh as well as you do.'

Father Huw brought food and wine and they sat under the trees in his garden while Urien, and Prior Robert, explained the reason for the visit. As they talked, villagers began to walk slowly past the garden, staring and listening with great interest. Brother John, bored with the endless talk, began to watch them. There were some very handsome girls among them, he noticed – that one passing now, for example, with long, silky brown hair . . .

'And you say the bishop has agreed?' Father Huw said doubtfully.

'Both bishop and prince,' said Prior Robert again, looking annoyed. 'And is Saint Winifred here, by your church?'

'Not here,' said Huw. 'She lies in the burial-ground of the old chapel, a mile or more from here. But . . .'

'But?' said Prior Robert.

'But this holy lady lived and died for the second time in this place,' said Huw. 'And although my people do not visit her grave or think of her often, they know that she is here among them and that they can depend on her. They are not going to like it if you take her bones away to England.'

'The opinions of the local people are surely not important,' said Prior Robert smoothly, 'when your bishop and your prince have agreed.'

'The people must be asked,' said Huw. 'I will arrange a meeting tomorrow after church.'

'He speaks the truth,' Urien told the prior. 'You will do well to get the agreement of the people of Gwytherin, however many blessings you already have.'

Prior Robert accepted the warning. 'Very well,' he said, and turned to Father Huw. 'I would like to go into your church to pray. Brother Cadfael will stay with you and help you with any arrangements you need to make. Brother John will take care of the horses. The rest will join me in prayers.'

He turned and went into the little stone church. Brother Richard, Brother Jerome, and Brother Columbanus followed him. As well as praying, they would plan how to persuade the people of Gwytherin to let them have the saint's bones.

'The prior and the sub-prior can stay in my house,' Father Huw told Cadfael. 'I shall sleep in the loft above my cow. This young brother and the horses can stay with Bened the blacksmith. Brother Cadfael, you and the other two can stay at Cadwallon's house, half a mile from here through the woods. He's one of the big land-owners round here.'

But Cadfael did not want to stay with Jerome and Columbanus. 'I'm the only one among us who can speak Welsh,' he said. 'It's best if I stay near to Prior Robert. Perhaps I could sleep in your loft, Huw.'

When it was all agreed, Urien prepared to leave. Cadfael walked up through the valley with him to the top of the hill, where Urien said goodbye and rode away on his horse.

Cadfael turned back and walked downhill towards the

river. He stopped under the trees to watch two men working in a field with oxen. The ploughman, walking behind the oxen, was short and dark, but the young ox-caller, walking backwards in front of the animals, was tall and golden-haired. He called to the oxen with kind and loving words, persuading them to do their best. It was clear that he loved them, and that they in turn worked hard to please him.

'He's a good caller,' thought Cadfael, 'but how did he come to Wales? If I'm not mistaken, he's English.'

Suddenly, not far away, a girl of eighteen or nineteen dropped lightly down from one of the trees. At first she did not see Cadfael, but when she did, she stared at him with interest. Cadfael stared back, just as interested. She was beautiful and richly dressed. Her long black hair fell wildly around her shoulders, and shone deep red where the sunlight caught it.

'You are one of the monks from Shrewsbury,' she said in perfect English.

'I am,' said Cadfael, surprised. 'But we've only just arrived. How did you find out about us so quickly?'

She smiled. 'Oh, everybody in Gwytherin knows all about you by now, and what you've come for. And Father Huw is right. We won't like it. Why do you want to take Saint Winifred away? It doesn't seem neighbourly or honest to me.'

She had chosen excellent words, he thought. 'I'm not completely happy about it myself,' he agreed sadly.

She looked at him carefully and, after a moment, said in Welsh, 'You must be the one who speaks our language.'

The girl stared at Cadfael with interest.

'Yes,' said Cadfael. 'I'm as Welsh as you, child. But I'm surprised that you speak English as well as I do.'

'Oh, no!' she said. 'I've only learned a very little.'

Cadfael then noticed that she was looking quickly and worriedly towards the river. The tall, fair young man – who Cadfael was certain was not a Welshman – had left the field and was walking through the water towards the tree where the girl had been hiding.

'I'm shy about my English. Please don't tell anyone!' said the girl. Her eyes gave Cadfael another message too.

'Of course I won't,' he said. Then, understanding her unspoken message, 'Well, I must go back now.'

'God go with you, Father,' she said, smiling thankfully.

'And with you, my child,' he answered.

He gave her a friendly smile and walked away, carefully choosing a route that avoided the fair young man. She watched him go, then turned happily to meet the young man.

'A Welsh girl of good family, meeting a young Englishman in secret, means trouble for someone,' thought Cadfael, as he walked back to Gwytherin. 'What I need now is a good, sensible, drinking companion, someone who knows every man, woman, and child in the valley.'

3

PRIOR ROBERT'S MISTAKE

adfael found two suitable companions that same evening. After prayers, he walked back to the blacksmith's house with Brother John. There were two men sitting outside Bened's door. Bened himself was a well-built, middle-aged man with a beard, and the other man was the ploughman who had followed the ox-team that day.

They made Cadfael welcome, and soon the drinking cups were going round. 'This is Cai, Rhisiart's ploughman,' Bened told Cadfael. 'Rhisiart is the biggest land-owner in the valley.'

'I saw you in the fields today,' Cadfael said to Cai. 'You have a good ox-team, and a good caller, too.'

'That's Engelard,' said Cai. 'Best caller I ever had.'

'I expect you've heard from Father Huw,' said Cadfael, 'about the meeting tomorrow after church. No doubt we will see Rhisiart there. Who else do you think will come?'

'Oh, Rhisiart will certainly be there!' said Cai, laughing. 'He always says what he thinks, but he's a good man.'

'And Cadwallon, his neighbour,' said Bened. 'He'll be there, too. But I don't know what either of them will have to say about the matter of Saint Winifred.'

Later, Cai and Cadfael walked back towards Father Huw's house together, and Cadfael learnt many useful things.

'Rhisiart's wife is dead,' Cai told him. 'He has no sons, so

17

his daughter, Sioned, will get house and land and everything. But she's beautiful too, and quick and clever. There's plenty of men who would like to marry her, but Rhisiart wants her to marry Peredur, Cadwallon's boy. He and Sioned grew up together, and Peredur will get all Cadwallon's land one day. What could please either father more? And the children seem perfectly matched, like brother and sister.'

'And does Sioned want to marry him?' asked Cadfael carefully, thinking that he had probably met the girl already.

'She likes him, but she won't think about marriage yet,' said Cai. 'Or perhaps she has plans of her own.' He looked at Cadfael carefully. 'You're not a man to speak carelessly, I'm sure. Sioned *has* got her eye on a man. One that wants her badly, but has no chance of ever getting her. Engelard! A good man with animals, worth plenty to Rhisiart, and Rhisiart knows it. But the boy's an Englishman! And he's running away from the English law. Oh, not for murder or anything terrible! For killing deer on another man's land. But he can't go back, not yet.'

'When did he come here?' asked Cadfael.

'Two years ago,' said Cai. 'Rhisiart gave him work and a little house to live in, and neither of them has ever had any reason to be sorry. But although Rhisiart likes Engelard, he will never allow an Englishman to marry his daughter.'

'Never,' agreed Cadfael.

'But Engelard hasn't stopped asking Rhisiart, and he never will. They're alike, those two. Both open and honest, but both determined to have what they want.'

'What does the girl say about it all?' asked Cadfael.

'Very little,' said Cai. 'She's waiting for the right moment.'

'And meanwhile, meeting her lover in the woods,' thought Cadfael. 'So that's how she learnt her English.'

* * *

Everyone in Gwytherin came to the church the next day. Father Huw stood outside with Cadfael and the younger monks, watching as people arrived and went into the church.

'Here's Rhisiart with his daughter,' he said to Cadfael. 'And the girl with Sioned is her servant, Annest.'

Rhisiart was a big, dark-haired man of about fifty, with a short beard. He had an honest face, with a quick smile and a friendly word for everyone he met. Sioned followed him, calmly and confidently, her black hair now smooth and tidy, not falling wildly around her shoulders, as when Cadfael had seen it in the woods. Her servant was also a handsome girl, and Brother John was staring at her long, silky brown hair, remembering her from the day before.

'Annest is the blacksmith's niece,' said Huw.

'Bened's niece?' Brother John said quickly. He watched her walk past – the shape of her waist, her shining hair . . .

'Lower your eyes, brother!' Jerome said to him. 'It's not nice to look at women like that!'

'And here comes Cadwallon, and his wife,' Huw told Cadfael. 'And his son, Peredur.'

Cadfael watched the tall, thin young man, and saw his eyes light up when he saw Sioned.

When the church was full, Prior Robert made his grand

19

Everyone in Gwytherin came to the church the next day.

entrance, and all the Shrewsbury brothers followed behind him into the church. The prayers began.

*   *   *

Only land-owners could take part in the meeting afterwards. The servants and the women moved away from the group standing outside the church – but not too far. They remained near enough to guess what was happening.

Father Huw told the men what the bishop and prince had

said about the saint's relics. Then Prior Robert spoke, with Cadfael translating his words into Welsh. The prior spoke movingly about the signs that Saint Winifred had sent them, but the Welsh faces around him were not enthusiastic.

'They're not happy!' Brother John whispered in Cadfael's ear.

He was right. The Welshmen talked among themselves in low voices, then Rhisiart stepped forward to speak.

'Saint Winifred is here, in Gwytherin!' he said. 'She is ours, not Bishop David's! Not the prince's! She lived here, and never said a word about wanting to leave us. Are we to believe that she wants to leave us *now*, after so long? Why has she never told us? Why?'

Others around him agreed loudly.

'Do you visit her?' said Prior Robert, his voice high and clear. 'Do you pray to her? Do you know any reason why she should want to remain here among you? Do you even take care of her grave?'

'We know that she's there,' said Rhisiart. 'We don't need to make a great noise about it. She doesn't ask us to come with prayers or tears, kneeling on the ground beside her! If she was unhappy here, she would tell us. *Us*, not a monk in a far-away abbey in England!'

'And the miracles that brought us here?' said Prior Robert.

'Miracles!' Rhisiart said. 'I think that was the devil talking to you! I do not believe that our saint would speak to you and not to us! And until she tells us that she wants to be moved, Saint Winifred stays here!'

21

Other voices shouted, 'Yes! That's right! She stays here!'

Prior Robert was angry, but he hid his anger well. There were many voices shouting against him, but he knew that it was just one man that he had to persuade. He lifted his hands and smiled at the crowd, then turned to Rhisiart.

'Rhisiart, let us go and speak calmly and quietly in Father Huw's house. And when I have said all that I want to say, I will not argue with you, whatever you decide.'

Rhisiart agreed to this, and followed the brothers and Father Huw into the house.

'I understand how the people of Gwytherin feel about losing Saint Winifred,' Prior Robert said to Rhisiart, 'but I'm sure that if you agree to it, they will follow you.'

Slowly, the prior put a small bag on the table and pushed it gently across until it rested against Rhisiart's right hand.

'I don't understand,' said Rhisiart. 'What is it?'

Cadfael knew at that moment that Prior Robert was making the biggest mistake of his life.

'It is yours,' Prior Robert said, 'if you persuade the people of Gwytherin to give us the saint.'

Too late he felt the awful coldness in the air, and realized what a terrible mistake he had made. Quickly, he tried to put it right. 'To use in any way you think best for Gwytherin, of course . . .'

But it was too late. The damage was done.

'Money!' said Rhisiart, angrily. 'You offer to *buy* our saint? You offer to buy *me*? To bribe me! Now I know that I was right to doubt you. I will tell my people—'

'I don't understand,' said Rhisiart. 'What is it?'

'No, wait!' The prior reached out and put a hand on Rhisiart's arm. 'You don't understand. If I was wrong to offer, I am sorry, indeed, I am sorry. But do not call it—'

Rhisiart pulled away. 'Tell him he need not be afraid,' he said to Cadfael. 'I should be ashamed to tell my people that a prior of Shrewsbury tried to bribe me.'

Father Huw put out a hand to prevent any of them trying to stop Rhisiart as he walked out of the house. 'Not now,' he said. 'He's angry now. Perhaps tomorrow something can be done, but not now.'

After a moment they went outside again and stood by the church while Rhisiart spoke to his people.

'I've listened to these men from Shrewsbury, and instead of changing my opinion, I am now a thousand times more

23

certain that I was right. Saint Winifred's place is here among us! It would be very wrong of us to allow these English foreigners to take her away to a strange place, and I strongly advise against it! And now this meeting is ended.'

*　*　*

Prior Robert did not apologize for his disastrous attempt to bribe Rhisiart, and his anger continued all afternoon. At last, after evening prayers, Father Huw made a suggestion.

'I will go to Rhisiart tonight, perhaps with Brother Cadfael, and ask him to come to my house tomorrow,' he said to the prior. 'Then, if between us we find some way to agree, another meeting of the people can be arranged.'

Prior Robert considered this. 'Very well,' he said. 'I hope you succeed.'

'It would look better if your messengers went on horses, Prior Robert,' said Cadfael, with a serious face. He could feel how restless Brother John was, and if they rode, Brother John would have to come too, to take care of the horses.

The prior agreed to this plan, and a little later Cadfael, Father Huw, and Brother John rode away into the trees.

'You're a good friend!' Brother John said to Cadfael. 'I'd had enough of all that, and now here we are, enjoying the quiet of the evening.'

As they arrived at Rhisiart's place, a voice called out to them. It was Cai, the ploughman.

'Hello, Cadfael!' he called. 'You're just in time for a drink or two! Bened's here with us tonight too.'

He and Bened were sitting on a seat outside one of the farm

buildings. Engelard sat near them in the shadows, and he moved along the seat to make room for Cadfael.

'Father Huw has come to talk peace,' Cadfael said, getting off his horse. 'And I must go with him. But look after Brother John while we talk, will you? He can speak English with Engelard.'

But Brother John had suddenly lost the use of his tongue in any language. He stood still, staring at the open door of Rhisiart's house where Annest was just coming out with a large jug in her hands. Her brown eyes looked at Cadfael and Huw with easy friendliness, but opened wide when she saw Brother John.

'Thirsty people, are you?' she said, still with one eye on Brother John. She put the jug down beside Cai, and sat down.

'Thirsty people, are you?' Annest said.

Brother John, like a man walking in his sleep, went and sat on the seat near her. Cadfael watched and smiled to himself, then followed Father Huw into the house.

* * *

'I will come,' Rhisiart said. 'Of course I will come, and listen to what Prior Robert has to say. But I expect very little from this meeting. If he wants me to change, he must change too. However, I'll come tomorrow at midday, or soon after.'

They collected Brother John and rode back through the woods to Father Huw's house, where the prior and the other three brothers received this message with worried faces.

'And will Rhisiart be persuaded?' asked Brother Richard. 'Will he listen to reason, and accept that he is wrong?'

Brother Jerome and Brother Columbanus watched Huw's face hopefully as they waited for his reply.

'He offers friendly interest and will consider whatever you have to say to him,' said Father Huw at last. 'I asked for no more than that.'

'He won't be easily persuaded,' said Cadfael. He looked at Prior Robert. 'Father Prior, you made a mistake this morning. You will need to undo that damage.'

* * *

Early next morning, Prior Robert gave his orders.

'Only Brother Richard and I, with Father Huw and Brother Cadfael, will meet with Rhisiart. You, Brother John, will make yourself useful and help to prepare the food. And you two, Brother Jerome, Brother Columbanus, will spend the hours praying to Saint Winifred. Ask for her blessing and help.

Go to the old chapel by the burial-ground where she is buried. Take food and wine with you, and stay there in prayer until I send for you.'

So Jerome and Columbanus took bread and meat, a jug of wine, and some water, and went off together.

It was a fine spring morning, but half an hour before midday there was a sharp shower of rain. By midday the sun was shining again. Perhaps Rhisiart had waited at Cadwallon's house until the rain stopped, they thought. But when he was an hour late, and there was no sign of him, Prior Robert said, 'He's afraid to come and see me!'

'No,' said Father Huw. 'Rhisiart keeps his promises.'

'I'll walk as far as Cadwallon's house,' Brother Richard said. 'Perhaps I'll meet him on the way.'

He was gone an hour and a half, and came back alone. 'I went a long way beyond Cadwallon's house, but saw no sign of him,' he said. 'On my way back I asked at Cadwallon's gate, but no one had seen him go past.'

'We'll wait until evening prayers,' said Prior Robert.

But Rhisiart did not come.

Five hours after midday, people began to arrive for evening prayers. On the forest path appeared not Rhisiart, but his daughter, dressed for church, and with Peredur behind her.

'Where is my father?' Sioned asked Cadfael as she arrived at the church door. 'Isn't he with you?'

Prior Robert understood the question before Cadfael could translate. 'Is she saying that Rhisiart left his house to come to our meeting?' he asked.

'Of course!' said Sioned. 'He left more than an hour before midday. He was going first to the hill fields, then through the woods down to the main forest path. Engelard was going with him as far as the fields. Where can he be?'

People were looking worried, and Father Huw said quickly, 'I think evening prayers must wait until we have found Rhisiart. Sioned will show us his route from the fields down to the forest path. Perhaps he's fallen and injured himself. Father Prior, will you come with us?'

'Of course,' said Prior Robert. 'We all will.'

Villagers and monks left the church and moved into the forest, searching to the left and right of the path. They were half a mile beyond Cadwallon's land when Father Huw suddenly put a hand on Cadfael's arm.

'Columbanus and Jerome are still at the old chapel! It's not far away. Shall we send someone to fetch them?'

'I'd forgotten them,' said the prior. 'Yes, send someone.'

One of the young village men hurried obediently away, and the searchers moved deeper into the forest.

It was Bened, crashing through the trees on the left of Cadfael, who shouted suddenly. Everyone stopped and looked towards the sound.

Cadfael ran, pushing through the branches until he reached an open circle of grass. Rhisiart was lying on his back, his arms open wide and his dead eyes staring up at the sky. There was an arrow through his heart.

4

AN ARROW IN THE HEART

At once Cadfael was on his knees, looking for signs of life in Rhisiart, but there were none. Then Sioned pushed her way through the circle of villagers. She gave a great cry and reached out towards her father, but Cadfael stopped her. 'No!' he said. 'Touch nothing! He has things to tell us.'

Something was worrying Cadfael. The grass where he knelt was still wet from the morning's shower. But under Rhisiart's right arm and side, it was dry. He felt outwards, the width of the body, to find the grass still dry. Strange!

'Saint Winifred has taken her revenge!' Prior Robert said loudly. 'Tell those who are against us, Cadfael, to be warned!'

The villagers stepped back, their faces white with fear. Those most afraid were on their knees, praying.

'No!' cried Peredur. 'A gentle saint does not take her revenge on a good man like Rhisiart. It's murder, Father Prior. A man's hand shot that arrow.'

Cadfael quickly translated, then added, 'The young man's right. This arrow wasn't shot from the sky. It was shot upwards, into the heart, perhaps with a short bow.'

'Saints can use men for their revenge,' said Robert darkly.

'The man would still be a murderer,' said Cadfael.

Then Bened said, 'I know this arrow. I know its owner. Look at this feather. It's blue on one side.'

A name was whispered round the circle. 'Engelard!'

'No!' cried Sioned. 'Engelard would cut off his own hand before allowing my father to die!'

'I'm not accusing him,' said Bened. 'But this is his arrow. And he's the best shot with the short bow in Gwytherin.'

'And everyone knows that he has argued often and angrily about . . . about . . .' someone began.

'About me,' said Sioned. 'Say what you mean!'

'We must find this young man, and ask him where he was when Rhisiart was killed,' said Prior Robert.

'You said that he and your father were going together as far as the fields, Sioned.' Huw looked round at the circle of faces. 'Did anyone see Rhisiart alive after that?'

There was silence. The crowd was getting bigger as people, hearing the news, came hurrying up from the village. Jerome and Columbanus had also arrived from the chapel.

'Engelard must be questioned,' said Prior Robert. 'It's clear that he had a motive for killing Rhisiart.'

'Motive?' said Sioned, angrily. 'What about *your* motive, Father Prior! Everyone knows that you want to take Saint Winifred away. And who was stopping you? My father!'

'Child!' cried Father Huw. 'Do not say these things to the prior! Every person in this valley knew that your father was coming to my house today, and the time. And many would know his route much better than these good brothers from Shrewsbury.' He turned to Prior Robert. 'Please forgive her, Father Prior! She speaks wildly, she doesn't know what she's saying.'

'I say no word of blame,' said the prior, coldly. 'Remind her that I've been with you and several others all day.'

But before Huw could speak, Sioned said, 'A man who would try to bribe my father would be quite willing to pay someone to do this work for him!'

'Take care!' shouted Robert. 'God will punish you!'

At that moment, they heard voices. Sioned recognized them, and a shadow of fear passed over her face. She looked round wildly, but there was no help. And then Annest and Engelard appeared from between the trees.

Engelard moved past Annest, his eyes fixed on Sioned's desperate face. Then he saw Rhisiart. His face went white. 'Dear God!' he whispered. He put an arm round Sioned, holding her close, then looked all round the watching faces.

'Who did this?'

At first, no one answered, then Sioned said, 'There are some here who are saying that *you* did.'

'Me?' he cried.

'No one here is accusing you, Engelard,' said Huw. 'But look carefully at the arrow that killed Rhisiart.'

Engelard moved closer to the body. 'It's one of mine!' He looked wildly round at the others. 'Do you really think I would kill, and then leave my arrow behind? And Rhisiart was my friend. He gave me work and a home after I escaped from England. I would never harm him.'

'He refused to let you marry his daughter,' said Bened.

'Perhaps you argued, and he made you angry,' said Huw. 'No one is saying that you planned this.'

'I've not had my bow with me all day,' said Engelard. 'And I left Rhisiart at the fields and did not see him again.'

Huw looked unhappy. 'Unless we can find someone who was with you or saw you at the time of Rhisiart's death, Engelard, then I'm afraid we must hold you until the prince's bailiff can question you.'

The men of Gwytherin agreed, and began to move forward in a line. All except Peredur, who moved back to the edge of the trees. Cadfael saw him staring hard at Sioned, sending her a silent message, which she whispered into Engelard's ear.

'Take hold of this man!' Prior Robert ordered.

But Engelard picked up a fallen branch from the ground and waved it around him in a circle, knocking two men down and sending the others running back. Then he jumped over the bodies, and made straight for the escape route that Peredur had left open.

'Stop him!' Huw shouted to Peredur.

Peredur jumped at Engelard, but seemed to trip and fall, and the young Englishman got past.

One of the villagers began to chase after him, and Brother John also started to run. The villager reached out and caught hold of Engelard's coat. At the same time, Brother John threw himself forward and caught the villager round the knees. Both men crashed to the ground – and Engelard pulled free. A second later, he had disappeared into the trees.

Brother John apologized to the villager, then looked at Prior Robert's angry face – but not before he had seen Annest looking at him with a warm smile and shining eyes.

Both men crashed to the ground – and Engelard pulled free.

'You have broken the laws of church and king!' said Prior Robert, white with anger. 'You should be ashamed!'

'I don't believe Engelard had any part in the killing,' said Brother John bravely. 'But I don't think he'll go far until he knows who did. And God help the murderer then! So I gave him his chance, and good luck to him! He's a good man.'

'You must answer to the prince's bailiff,' Prior Robert said coldly. 'Brother Cadfael, ask Father Huw if there is a safe prison where this brother can be held.'

Brother John began to look around and plan his own escape, but then he heard Cadfael say, 'Father Huw suggests Sioned's house, if she will allow it.' Hearing this, Brother John mysteriously lost all interest in immediate escape.

*　*　*

The men of Gwytherin cut young branches from the trees and made a bed to carry Rhisiart's body home.

'Where is Peredur?' asked Sioned. She was calmer now. 'I thought he would want to help carry my father.' She walked behind her father's body, with Cadfael beside her. 'Did my father tell you the things he had to tell?' she asked quietly.

'Some,' said Cadfael. 'Keep the clothes he is wearing, and tell me where they're wet and where they're dry. I'll come to you tomorrow, as soon as I can.'

'I must know the truth,' she said. 'I'm glad you're here. You don't believe it was Engelard.'

'I'm almost certain it was not,' said Cadfael. 'He's taller than your father. How could he shoot an arrow *upwards* into a man who was shorter than him? Kneeling down? I doubt it.

And Engelard did not hate Rhisiart. I know that.' He smiled at her. 'You know where he is. You have more than one secret place, I'm sure. But tell me nothing, unless you need somebody to take a message.'

'You can take a message to Peredur for me. Thank him for what he did, and tell him that I was sorry he was not here to carry my father home,' she said. 'Then come tomorrow.'

* * *

As Cadfael was walking back to Huw's with the other brothers, he saw Peredur in the woods near his father's house, and gave him Sioned's message. 'She was sorry that you were not there to help carry her father home,' he said.

'There were plenty of her own people there,' said Peredur. 'She did not need me.'

'No, but she thinks of you like a brother,' said Cadfael.

'It's not her brother that I wanted to be,' said Peredur.

'No, I understand that,' said Cadfael. 'But you behaved like one when you helped Engelard. And Rhisiart—'

'Please!' cried Peredur. 'Don't say any more!'

'I'm sorry,' said Cadfael. 'I know this is painful for you. Sioned told me you were fond of her father—'

The boy gave a sharp cry, and turned and ran away into the trees. Cadfael watched him for a moment, then walked thoughtfully back to his companions.

* * *

'You and I,' said Bened, when Cadfael walked down to the blacksmith's that evening, 'must drink alone tonight. Cai has a new job as a prison-keeper at Rhisiart's place.'

'You mean Brother John has *Cai* for his keeper?'

'That's right,' said Bened. 'And my niece Annest will take him food. So you needn't worry about Brother John.'

'I wasn't worried about him at all,' said Cadfael dryly.

Bened put a jug of wine on the table. 'I was glad when Engelard got away,' he said. 'I can't believe he's a murderer.'

'Sioned said what other people are probably thinking,' said Cadfael. 'We came here for a saint's relics, and Rhisiart stopped us. What could be more natural than to suspect one of us? But all six of us were together until after morning prayers. Then Prior Robert, Brother Richard and I were with Father Huw until Brother Richard went to look for Rhisiart. He was gone an hour and a half, and didn't talk to anyone until he asked about Rhisiart at Cadwallon's gate. I must ask the gate-man if he remembers. And Brother Jerome and Brother Columbanus were in the chapel praying, until Father Huw sent somebody to fetch them just before we found Rhisiart's body. So we all, except for Richard, have alibis.'

'But a holy man would never murder anyone!' said Bened.

'Holy men are just as weak or as strong as other men, my friend,' said Cadfael sadly.

He walked back to Huw's loft alone after leaving Bened. His thoughts turned to Peredur. Earlier, the young man had run away when Cadfael spoke about Rhisiart. Like a murderer? 'He looked like a man being chased by a devil,' thought Cadfael. 'But *that* devil? No, I can't believe it. Rhisiart *wanted* him to marry Sioned, so why kill him?'

* * *

When the five monks met the next morning, outside the church, Cadfael noticed that Brother Columbanus looked very unhappy. He soon discovered the reason.

'Father Prior,' said Columbanus, miserably. 'Yesterday you sent Brother Jerome and me to the chapel. After eating our meal, we knelt down to pray. But – oh, Father, I am so sorry – I fell asleep! I think I slept all afternoon! The next thing I remember is Brother Jerome shaking my shoulder and telling me that a messenger was calling us to go with him.' A tear fell from his eye. 'Don't blame Brother Jerome. He didn't know that I was asleep.'

Only Cadfael's quick eyes noticed the look of fear that passed across Brother Jerome's face. Was it fear of blame for not waking his companion? Or something else? Columbanus, Cadfael thought, had been Jerome's alibi for the time of the killing. But now? How could a sleeping man be an alibi?

'Brother,' Prior Robert said to Columbanus, in his kindly and forgiving voice, 'your mistake was human, and—'

But at that moment, Father Huw hurried up to them. 'I've come to tell you there's been another meeting,' he said. 'The villagers heard your warning about the saint's revenge, and most of them believed it. So they have agreed to let you take Saint Winifred's relics. They now believe it is God's wish.'

It was everything Prior Robert had hoped for. 'I am certain,' he said, 'that the people of Gwytherin are right.'

'They're not happy about losing the saint,' said Father Huw, 'but they won't stop you. We'll take you to her grave. Will you break the ground today?'

'No,' said Prior Robert, after thinking for a moment. 'There shall be three nights of prayer in the chapel, to make sure that what we are doing is right and has God's blessing. There are six of us here, if you will join us, Father Huw. Each night, two of us will watch and pray all night long.'

* * *

Later, Cadfael went to visit Sioned and found her sitting beside her father's body in a small private room. She got up to meet him, with a sad smile.

'I'm glad you're here. I have his clothes for you,' she said.

As Cadfael expected, Rhisiart's clothes were damp on the back but dry on the front. 'You remember how he was lying when we found him?' said Cadfael.

'I shall remember it all my life,' said Sioned, her voice shaking. 'His legs half-turned, like . . .' She stopped.

'Like a man who had been lying on his face but who was pulled over onto his back,' Cadfael finished for her.

Sioned stared at him. 'Tell me your thoughts.'

'First,' said Cadfael, 'remember where this happened. A place surrounded by trees. Plenty of hiding places, yes, but would a man with a bow and arrow choose a place like that? No – if he's too close, he can't take a careful aim.'

'That's right,' said Sioned.

'I don't like this arrow. Why was it there?' said Cadfael. 'So that people would suspect Engelard? Perhaps, but I can't get it out of my head that there's another reason, too.'

'To kill!' said Sioned.

'Do you think so? Look at his shirt – the blood is all at the back, not at the front where the arrow entered,' said Cadfael. 'And when I knelt beside him, the grass was wet under him, but dry all down his right side. Now there was half an hour of rain yesterday morning. When that rain began, *your father*

'I don't like this arrow. Why was it there?' said Cadfael.

was lying on his face, already dead. And that's why that piece of grass remained dry – because his body was lying on it.'

'And then,' Sioned said slowly, 'somebody turned him over onto his back. But the arrow entered his chest. How could he then fall onto his face?'

'I don't know,' said Cadfael. 'Nor why he bled behind and not in front. Sioned, may I look closely at his body?'

'Yes,' said Sioned. 'I'll help you.' Her eyes burned with anger. 'At least you and I are not afraid to touch him. We have no fear that he'll bleed again to accuse *us* of his murder.'

Cadfael looked at her. 'True!' he said thoughtfully. 'But many people do believe the dead can bleed again.'

'Don't you believe it?' said Sioned, surprised.

'I think all or most of the brothers believe it. But I've seen too many dead men picked up after a battle by those who killed them, and not one of them bled fresh blood. Child, what I believe or don't believe is not important. But what the murderer believes may be.' Cadfael looked back at the body. 'Now, we must turn him to look at the other wound.'

They lifted the body onto its right side, and Cadfael looked at the wound high on the left side of the back.

'We took the arrow out from the front of his chest,' said Sioned. 'So why all that blood? The arrow only just broke the skin on his back.'

But there was another cut, above the arrow hole.

'A wound, I suspect, made by a long, thin, sharp knife,' said Cadfael. 'It was from there that his life-blood came out. That was why he fell on his face, and why, afterwards, he was turned on his back. The arrow went into his chest *after he was dead*, to hide the fact that he was killed with a knife. But the arrow was not shot from a bow. It was *pushed up* into his chest, after a knife had been used to open the way.'

'The same knife that killed him?' said Sioned, her face white but her voice calm.

'Probably. Then the arrow was pushed in afterwards.'

'Engelard's arrow!' said Sioned. 'But my father was not turned over onto his back until after the rain had stopped – half an hour later. Why did the murderer wait so long between killing, and pushing in the arrow?' Her eyes burned in her white face as she stared at Cadfael. '*Who is this man?* He knows my father's movements. He knows where to find Engelard's arrows. He wants God knows what from my father's death, but certainly he wants Engelard to carry the blame for it. Brother Cadfael, who is he? *Who?*'

'With God's help, Sioned,' said Cadfael, 'you and I will find out. At the moment I have no answers. But, as you said, many people believe that the dead bleed again when touched by their murderer's hand. This may help us get the answers we want. Now listen, this is what you must do . . .'

5

PEREDUR TELLS THE TRUTH

After evening prayers, Father Huw and the brothers went up to the old chapel, all six together. And there, coming to meet them, was another group of people – Rhisiart's servants, carrying Rhisiart's body on its bed of green branches, and in front of them walked Sioned, dressed in dark clothes. Her face was calm and proud, her eyes full of sadness.

She stopped in front of Prior Robert. 'I hear that you are going to watch and pray for three nights before you take Saint Winifred with you,' she said. 'My father meant her no harm, and I want her to know that. Will you allow him to lie in her chapel for those three nights? And will those praying there say one prayer for him? Is that too much to ask?'

Prior Robert was not all bad. 'It is a fine and daughterly thing that you ask,' he said gently. 'And gladly I agree.'

So Rhisiart's body, covered in a white sheet, was placed next to the reliquary waiting for Saint Winifred's bones.

'Each morning I shall come to give thanks to those who prayed for my father during the night,' said Sioned.

Then she went away without another word.

Father Huw and Brother Jerome spent the first night in the chapel. In the morning, Prior Robert and his companions arrived to find Sioned, Annest and some of the villagers waiting. The monks and the two young women went inside, and the people of Gwytherin filled the doorway after them.

'It was a quiet night,' said Father Huw. 'We have prayed, child, and I believe that we have been heard.'

'I am grateful,' said Sioned. 'Will you do one more thing? Will you put your hand on my father's heart, each of you, and say one more prayer?'

'Gladly!' said Father Huw, and stepped forward.

Brother Jerome hesitated. He looked at Prior Robert. Cadfael watched both their faces carefully, wondering. Had Robert sent his obedient follower to take Rhisiart's life?

The prior thought, then said, 'You may do what she asks.'

Brother Jerome stepped forward readily and put his hand on Rhisiart's heart. And no fresh blood came through the sheet to accuse him. But what, thought Cadfael, does that tell us? Is he, or the man who gave the order, the one to blame?

The next night did not go as planned. Late in the evening, Prince Owain's bailiff arrived in Gwytherin. He wanted to ask Prior Robert many questions about Rhisiart's death and Brother John's crime, so the prior could not pray at the chapel that night. Brother Richard spent the night there alone, and the next morning he calmly put his hand on Rhisiart's heart and said a prayer. But nothing happened.

The third night, Cadfael and Brother Columbanus went to the chapel. Cadfael knelt at the prayer-desk and made himself comfortable. He said a prayer for Rhisiart, and for all those people who were unhappy because of this little saint.

It was nearly midnight when he heard strange noises coming from Columbanus. The young man's eyes were open, and his lips were moving in a quiet song. Suddenly, he threw his head back and gave a great cry. Then he fell forward on to the floor with his arms and legs out straight.

Cadfael got up and hurried to him. He shook the young man's shoulder, but Columbanus' eyes remained closed, and there was a happy, peaceful look on his face.

'Now what am I supposed to do?' thought Cadfael. 'Let him sleep, I suppose. He looks comfortable, and his breathing is deep and regular. He won't come to any harm.'

It was a long night, and Cadfael found that it was impossible to think or pray. Sioned was the first to enter the chapel in the morning, and Prior Robert, the other monks, and Annest came in behind her.

Sioned gave a sharp cry when she saw Columbanus. 'Is he dead?' she asked.

Prior Robert pushed past her. 'Brother Cadfael! What happened here?'

'He's not dead, nor is he in any danger,' said Cadfael. 'At midnight he suddenly stood up and fell forward with a cry. Since then, he has slept peacefully.'

'Perhaps he has had another vision,' said Brother Richard. 'Shall we carry him to Father Huw's house, so that he is near the church? When he wakes, he may want to pray.'

So Columbanus was carried through the forest to Father Huw's house. Cadfael let them go. He turned to look at Sioned and saw that she was looking at him. Without speaking, he stepped forward and put his hand on the dead man's heart and said a prayer.

Sioned walked beside him as they followed the others.

'What more can we do?' she said. 'We've learned nothing yet, and today my father will be buried.'

'I know,' said Cadfael. They walked on silently, then Cadfael said, 'When you bury your father, be sure that Peredur comes with *his* father.'

*   *   *

Later, when the bell rang for prayers, Columbanus got up from the bed. His eyes were open but he walked out of Huw's house, into the church and knelt down like a man who was still asleep. The church was full, and there were more people outside the door. The news had gone round that something strange and wonderful had happened at Saint Winifred's chapel, and that a message from Saint Winifred herself was expected after morning prayers.

And at the end, when Prior Robert was moving towards the door, Brother Columbanus suddenly began to speak in a high voice:

'Oh, Father, I have seen wonders! At midnight I heard a sweet voice call my name, and suddenly there was a soft, golden light. In the middle of the light appeared a beautiful woman, and all around her was a cloud of white petals from sweet-smelling flowers. "I am Winifred," she said. "I have come to bless your plans, and to forgive those who were against them." And then – oh, wonderful! – she put her hand on Rhisiart's heart and said a prayer, forgiving him!'

'These are great wonders indeed!' said Prior Robert.

'There's more, Father! "When my bones are taken out of

45

the ground," she said, "there will be an open grave. In this grave let Rhisiart be buried. And let him rest in peace.'"

* * *

Nearly everybody in Gwytherin came to watch the opening of Saint Winifred's grave. Sioned and all her servants were at the grave-side. Bened and Cadwallon were there. And Peredur, who clearly wished he was a hundred miles away.

The grave was deep. By mid-afternoon the diggers had almost disappeared from view. Suddenly Cadfael knelt and began to dig with his fingers. After a minute or two, he took an arm-bone from the ground.

'She is here,' he said. 'But we must be careful, or her bones will turn to dust. Leave her to me now.'

Gently, Cadfael found and moved every bone, until Saint Winifred was there for all to see. The reliquary was brought out from the chapel, and the bones placed gently inside it. When the lid was closed and fastened, Prior Robert said prayers, and the people of Gwytherin watched in silence.

'Now it is time to bury Rhisiart,' said Father Huw.

After the burial prayers were finished, the body was carried out to the grave. Sioned took a silver cross from her neck. She was standing near Cadwallon and Peredur, so it was simple and natural for her to turn towards them.

'Peredur, you were like a son to my father. Will you put this cross on his chest, where the murderer's arrow killed him? It's my last present to him, and it can be yours, too.'

Peredur could not speak. He stared at her face and then at the silver cross. Every eye watched him. How could he refuse?

But how could he do what she asked without touching the dead man? He took the cross from her and stepped towards the body. His hands shook and his face was white. Suddenly he stopped, not able to go forward or back.

'Come, son,' said Father Huw, quietly. 'Don't keep the dead waiting. Remember, Rhisiart was like a father to you.'

But Peredur could not move. He fell down on to his knees. One hand held the cross and the other hid his face.

Peredur fell down on to his knees.

'He cannot accuse me!' he cried. 'I did not murder him! I did what I did when Rhisiart was already dead!'

There was a sudden, sharp intake of breath from all those around the grave, and then everyone was silent, watching, and waiting. At last, Peredur went on.

'I did not kill Rhisiart,' he said, trying to make his voice calm. 'I – I found him dead.'

'When did you find him?' asked Brother Cadfael.

'I went out after the rain stopped,' said Peredur. 'Soon after midday. I was going up to the field. I found him in that place where we all saw him later. He was dead then, you must believe me! There was nothing I could do for him, but . . .' He looked at the ground, and his voice was low and ashamed. 'I knew that Sioned would never marry me while Engelard was here, and I knew that people would believe Engelard had killed Rhisiart, if – if there was proof . . .'

'Did *you* believe it?' asked Cadfael, softly.

'No!' said Peredur. 'Of course not!'

'You were willing to let people accuse him, and—'

'I thought he would run away, back to England,' said Peredur. 'And then perhaps Sioned would do what her father wanted her to do, and marry me.'

'So you stole one of Engelard's arrows,' said Cadfael.

'No, I didn't steal it,' said Peredur. 'I had one with me. I picked it up by mistake when I went shooting with Engelard last week.' His face was calm at last. He had spoken, and the worst was over. Now he went on to tell the rest of it. 'Rhisiart was murdered with a knife, but the knife wasn't there. I turned him over onto his back. Then, with my own knife, I opened the way for the arrow and put it in.' He put a hand up to his eyes. 'And I've not had one quiet moment, night or day, since then.'

Everyone was quiet. The truth fell like thunder, silencing them all. Rhisiart had not been shot down with an arrow, but killed from behind with a knife. That was the way a coward kills, not the way a holy saint takes revenge.

Father Huw broke the silence. 'Peredur, you know that you must be punished,' he said.

'I *want* to be punished!' said Peredur. 'I cannot live with myself unless I am.'

'I will speak to the prince's bailiff,' said Father Huw. 'Now go home and wait until I send for you.'

Peredur turned to Sioned. 'May I do what you asked me to do?' he said. 'I'm not afraid now. Your father was a good man. He will not accuse me of something I did not do.'

'Yes,' she said. 'I still want you to do it.'

Peredur went forward and dropped on to his knees beside Rhisiart's body. He put his hand, and then Sioned's cross, on Rhisiart's heart. No fresh blood came from the dead man.

After a moment, Peredur stood up and walked away. People moved back to make a path for him. Cadwallon, his face white and miserable, went after his son.

6

THE BOTTLE OF POPPY MEDICINE

It was now too late in the day for Prior Robert and his companions to take the relics and leave for Shrewsbury. 'We will stay here tonight,' the prior said, 'and after evening prayers one of us will again watch the night through with Saint Winifred in her chapel. And if the prince's bailiff asks us to stay longer, then we will. There's still the matter of Brother John, who is in trouble with the law.'

'The bailiff is more interested in finding Rhisiart's murderer,' said Father Huw. 'But I must go to Peredur's home now, and do what I can for his poor parents.'

The people of Gwytherin began to move quietly away, while two of Rhisiart's men filled in the grave. It was soon finished. Then Sioned turned towards the gate, and all the rest of her people followed. Cadfael walked along beside her.

'Tomorrow you will go back to Shrewsbury,' she said. 'And Engelard must go on hiding. We know now why Peredur used Engelard's arrow. But does that prove Engelard did not kill my father, perhaps after a terrible argument?'

'With a knife in the *back*?' said Cadfael. 'Never!'

Sioned smiled. 'All that proves is that you know him. Not everyone does, and those people may say that perhaps Peredur was right after all, without knowing it. Perhaps Engelard *was* the killer.'

Cadfael knew that she was right.

'There is also Brother John to consider,' said Sioned. Was it Annest, walking behind her, who reminded her with a gentle touch on the arm?

'I've not forgotten Brother John,' said Cadfael.

'But perhaps the bailiff has,' suggested Sioned. 'Hasn't he enough trouble here to keep him busy? Surely he'll look the other way if Brother John goes home with the rest of you.'

'And if he *thought* that Brother John had gone back to Shrewsbury, would he forget about him?' said Cadfael. 'And ask no questions about one more Englishman living and working here?' He was remembering a conversation with Bened, who had said that Brother John would make an excellent blacksmith – if given the chance.

'I always knew you were quick,' said Sioned, smiling.

'I'm not afraid for John,' said Cadfael. 'I'm more worried about Engelard. Send your people home and stay the night with Annest at Bened's house. And if God helps me with some new thought, I'll come to you there.'

They were now a long way behind Prior Robert and the others, and as they passed the gate to Cadwallon's land, a worried-looking Father Huw came hurrying out.

'Brother Cadfael, will you help me here?' he said. 'You understand medicines, perhaps you can advise . . .'

'Peredur's mother!' whispered Sioned. 'Whenever there's trouble, she cries and cries until she makes herself ill. You'd better go in alone. If she sees me, she'll cry even more.'

Cadfael could hear Peredur's mother screaming and crying

even before he entered the little room where her husband and son were trying to calm her.

'Mother,' Peredur was saying, 'nobody blames you, and nobody will. Everyone in Gwytherin will feel sorry for you. It is I who must be punished, not you.'

His mother gave another loud scream and threw her arms around him. 'No! No! I won't let them!' she cried. 'You're my own son, and I won't let them do it!' And when he pulled away, she shouted that he was cruel and wanted to kill her – and then began to scream with laughter.

Cadfael took Peredur to one side. 'Be sensible, boy, and get out of her sight. You're only making things worse. Now, Columbanus and Jerome have gone on to the church with the prior, so you must show me where they sleep. Columbanus brought some of my poppy medicine with him, in case he had another fit. But he's not had any reason to use it.'

'What does it do?' asked Peredur. He was tired and his hands were shaking.

'It calms a person, and kills pain,' said Cadfael.

'I could use some of that myself!' said Peredur.

In the brothers' room, Cadfael soon found the small green bottle he was looking for. He held it up to the light. Instead of being full, the bottle was three-quarters empty.

How strange! He stared at it. 'Enough gone to put a man to sleep for hours!' he thought. 'And now that I think back . . . there was at least one time when a man slept away hours of the day instead of watching and praying. The day Rhisiart died, Columbanus failed to do what he was told to do.

'Enough gone to put a man to sleep for hours!'

Columbanus, who had the medicine and knew its use . . .'

'What must we do?' asked Peredur, worried by the silence. 'If it tastes unpleasant, she won't drink it.'

'We'll put it in some strong wine,' said Cadfael.

Peredur's mother was still crying, but less violently now. Cadfael quickly gave her the cup of medicine, saying, 'Drink this!' She drank it automatically. And slowly, as Cadfael, Huw, and Cadwallon watched, she became calm.

'Get her to bed,' Cadfael told Cadwallon. 'She'll sleep through the night. And let your son rest, too. Father Huw will take care of him now.' He turned to Huw, who was looking very grateful. 'I'll see you at evening prayers, Huw,' said Cadfael. 'I've things to do at Bened's house first.'

The empty bottle was heavy in Cadfael's pocket and his thoughts were busy. Before he reached Bened's house, he had decided what must be done, but did not know how to do it.

Cai and Bened were sitting together on the seat outside the house, with a jug of wine in front of them.

'So,' said Bened, 'the mystery still isn't solved.'

'There's still tonight before we leave for Shrewsbury,' said Cadfael. 'I must speak with Sioned. We've things to do, and not much time for doing them.'

'Have a drink with us first,' said Cai. 'It takes no time at all, and it will help you think.'

The jug was still half full when Annest ran in through the gate at full speed. 'Don't just sit there drinking!' she cried. 'The prince's bailiff is having supper with the monks at Father Huw's house, and I heard them talking. He's coming to our house to take Brother John away to prison!'

They all jumped to their feet. 'All right, girl,' said Cai. 'I'll get Brother John to a safe place before the bailiff gets near us. I'll take one of your horses, Bened.'

'Get one for me,' said Annest. 'I'm coming with you.'

'What else did you hear them say?' Cadfael asked her.

'They were deciding who was going to watch and pray in the chapel tonight,' said Annest. 'The fair one – the one who has visions – is going. Columbanus, that's his name.'

'He'll be there alone, will he?' said Cadfael, thoughtfully.

'So I heard,' said Annest. Cai was coming with the horses, and Annest stood up. 'Brother Cadfael,' she said, 'do you think it's wrong for me to love John? Or for him to love me?'

'No,' said Cadfael. 'Everyone should be allowed to make one new beginning. John made a mistake when he became a monk. I don't think he's making a mistake this time.'

He watched her ride away, then went inside to see Sioned. He told her where Annest had gone, then said, 'They'll take care of John. But we have things to do, and no time to lose.'

'You've found out something,' she said, watching him.

He told her what had happened at Cadwallon's house, and what he wanted her to do. 'I know you can speak English, and you must speak it tonight,' he said. 'This may be dangerous, but I'll be near you. And you can tell Engelard to come, but he must promise to stay hidden.'

'I'm not afraid,' said Sioned. 'I'll do anything.'

'Then sit down and learn your part well,' said Cadfael.

* * *

Later that evening, Prior Robert and Brother Richard rode to Rhisiart's house with the prince's bailiff between them. The bailiff's two men and Brother Cadfael rode behind.

The bailiff was annoyed. This was Prior Robert's idea, not his. He wanted to send the Benedictine brothers and their problems back to Shrewsbury.

There was nobody at the gate, which was strange, and people were running here, there, and everywhere. Then a handsome young woman ran towards them. 'Oh, sirs, excuse me, but the gate-man was called away to help in the search . . . What can I do for you? My lady is resting, but can I—?'

'We've come to take away your prisoner,' said the bailiff. 'A young brother from Shrewsbury Abbey.'

'Oh, sir!' said Annest. 'It's true we had a brother here—'

'Had?' said Prior Robert sharply.

'Had?' said the bailiff thoughtfully.

'He's gone, sir!' said Annest. 'He escaped when one of our men took him his supper. We have men looking for him in the forest now, but I think he's got away!'

Cai appeared at just the right moment. He had a white bandage round his head, and walked with shaky steps.

'Oh, sir!' said Annest. 'It's true we had a brother here—'

'This is the poor man who took the prisoner his supper,' said Annest. 'He was knocked on the head.'

The bailiff questioned Cai, and all the other servants, who tried to be helpful but only confused matters even more. Prior Robert got angrier and angrier.

'Well, it's clear your young man has got away,' said the bailiff calmly. He noticed the light in the handsome young woman's eyes, and hid a smile. 'We cannot blame anyone; they didn't expect violence from a Benedictine brother. We must look somewhere else for our escaped prisoner.'

Prior Robert was shaking with anger, but there was nothing he could do. 'Well, I must leave for Shrewsbury tomorrow,' he said. 'We can't stay here any longer, so I must leave you to punish Brother John.'

'I'll do whatever needs to be done *when* we find him,' said the bailiff. He did not seem at all worried about it.

'And when he has completed his punishment, will you return him to us?' said Prior Robert.

'*When* he has, yes,' said the bailiff. He smiled kindly at the prior. 'But a lot of runaways are never found, you know.'

7

A VISION IN THE NIGHT

Brother Columbanus entered the small, dark chapel and closed the door gently behind him. A small light burned inside, and there were shadows all around Saint Winifred's reliquary. Beyond the light, everything was dark.

Columbanus moved a prayer-desk to the centre of the chapel, facing the saint's coffin. He was here to watch for the night, but there was nobody to watch *him*, so he made himself comfortable on his knees, put his head on his arms, and was soon asleep.

It was almost midnight when he began to dream that a woman was calling his name, slowly and clearly, over and over again: 'Columbanus . . . Columbanus . . .'

He opened his eyes and stared wildly. It was darker than earlier. The light seemed to be half-hidden behind the coffin. And the voice of his dream was still with him, whispering out of the darkness, very soft, very low, but clear as a bell . . .

'Columbanus, Columbanus, what have you done? You have been false to me, you have lied, and you have murdered. What can you say to Winifred now? I never wanted to leave my resting-place here in Gwytherin. I sent a good man to speak for me, and today he was buried here. Why,' the voice whispered coldly, 'have you killed my servant Rhisiart?'

Columbanus could not move or find his voice.

58

'Columbanus, murderer! Speak! Tell me the truth!'

'I never touched Rhisiart!' Columbanus cried at last. 'I was here, in your holy chapel all that afternoon. But I slept—'

'You are lying! It was not you who slept,' the voice said, angry now. 'Who put poppy medicine in the wine? Brother Jerome slept, not you! *You* went out into the forest and waited for Rhisiart, and killed him!'

'No, no!' cried Columbanus, shaking with fear. 'I was asleep here when Father Huw's messenger came for us. Jerome woke me . . . the messenger saw us . . .'

'The messenger never passed the doorway. Brother Jerome was already waking up, and went to meet him. You lied then, and you're lying now. Jerome did not know, but *I* know! And I will take my revenge if you lie to me once more!'

'No!' screamed Columbanus. 'I'm not lying. I never harmed Rhisiart! I never put Jerome to sleep!'

'Then what is this?'

Something crashed on to the floor, and at the same moment the light went out. Sick with fear, Columbanus moved forward and felt bits of glass under his hands and knees. He could smell poppy medicine, and knew that he was kneeling among the broken pieces of the green bottle.

When his eyes were used to the darkness, he could see a shape. Between him and the coffin, someone was standing, a woman, the head and shoulders lit by the starlight from a high window. He had not seen her come, he had heard nothing. She was covered from head to foot in white, Saint Winifred in her grave clothes, her arm out in front of her, pointing at him.

59

He tried to make himself small on the floor. 'I did it for you!' he cried. 'For you and for my abbey! I believed that you wanted it – that God wanted it! But Rhisiart would not let you go. So I gave the medicine to Jerome, in his wine, and when he was sleeping, I went out into the forest and waited for Rhisiart. I followed him. I killed him. Oh, Saint Winifred, don't punish me for killing your enemy . . .'

'In the back!' came the whisper, as cold as ice. Then louder, 'In the back! The way a coward kills! In the back! Say it!'

'In the back! Yes! But it was all for you, I did it for you!'

'You did it for yourself,' accused the voice. 'For your own glory. To show yourself as God's favourite, the holiest of the brothers, and so one day to become the youngest abbot in the country. You will do anything to get what you want.'

'No, no!' he shouted. As she moved nearer to him, he pulled himself to his feet, beating at her blindly, trying to keep her away. His hand caught the sheet – and pulled it from her face and head. Dark hair fell round her shoulders. His fingers touched soft smooth skin instead of hard bones.

He was very quick, Columbanus. It took him only seconds to realize that this was a real woman, and who she was, and how she had trapped him. And only seconds more to realize that she was alone, and that she must not live to tell others. She must die, and disappear, and he would still be safe.

But Sioned was almost as quick as he was. She felt the change in him, from terrible fear to murderous anger, and jumped away. He came after her, lifting his arm, and she saw the starlight shine on a long thin knife in his hand.

'The same knife that killed my father!' she thought.

Suddenly a door opened somewhere. Wind blew through the chapel, a loud voice shouted, and Brother Cadfael came running towards them like a thunderstorm. Columbanus let go of Sioned and she fell against the wall, his knife cutting her arm. Then he turned and ran.

Cadfael put his arms around Sioned. 'Why did you get near him? I *told* you to—'

'Go after him,' shouted Sioned. 'Do you want him to get away? He killed my father!'

They ran to the door together, but Cadfael was out first, into the starlit night. She ran close behind him, down the narrow path, through the burial ground towards the gate.

A man jumped out of the trees beyond the wall, and ran to the gateway. Columbanus saw him, paused for a second, then ran on, straight at the shadow that moved to stop him.

'Be careful, Engelard!' shouted Sioned. 'He has a knife!'

Engelard heard her, and jumped to the right. Columbanus ran past him, but Engelard's long left arm went round the monk's neck. Columbanus turned and hit out wildly with his knife. Engelard caught his wrist and bent it back, and a second later, the knife dropped to the ground. Both men jumped after it but Engelard got there first, and threw the knife into the trees. Then he held Columbanus, trapping the monk's arms to his sides.

'Is this the man?' he asked.

'Yes,' said Sioned. 'It's my father's murderer.'

Engelard saw the blood coming from her left arm, and the

*They ran to the door together, but Cadfael was out first,
into the starlit night.*

blood on the white sheet around her. Suddenly, everything Engelard saw seemed to be blood-red. This was the man who had murdered Rhisiart, Engelard's good friend. And now he had tried to kill Sioned!

'You dirty coward!' shouted Engelard. 'Murderer! Coward!' He lifted Columbanus from the ground and shook him violently by the neck, over and over again. Then he threw him down at his feet in the grass.

'Get up, you coward!' he shouted. 'And fight!'

But Columbanus did not move. Cadfael knelt down beside him and gently shook his shoulder. Then he put a hand inside the young monk's habit, on his chest, and put an ear against Columbanus' half-open mouth. After a moment or two, he looked up at Engelard and Sioned.

'His neck is broken,' said Cadfael. 'He's dead.'

They stared at the young monk.

'He can't be dead,' said Engelard doubtfully. 'I only shook him. Nobody dies as easily as that.'

'This one did,' said Cadfael.

'We must go to Father Huw and your prior,' said Engelard, 'and tell them exactly what happened. I didn't mean to kill him, but . . .'

He did not expect any blame. Cadfael understood this. But he also knew what damage this could do to their young lives. With Columbanus dead, how strong was their proof that the monk had killed Rhisiart?

'We'll carry him into the chapel,' said Cadfael. 'Sioned, find his knife. Then we'll put a bandage round your arm.'

They did what he told them without question. Engelard washed and bandaged Sioned's arm. But then he repeated his opinion that they must tell the whole story to the prior.

'But they won't believe us,' said Cadfael. 'If Columbanus was still alive, we could make him say again what he said tonight. But he's dead, and Prior Robert, the prince, the bishop – the whole world! – will refuse to believe he was a murderer. They'll say that this is a killing by a desperate man. A man already wanted for another murder, and trying to escape both together. No, you must forget any idea about telling anyone the true story. We must use the rest of the night to find a better way. Now, clear away the broken glass while I think. There must be no signs left.'

Obediently they began to tidy up and left him to think.

After a while Cadfael looked at Sioned. 'When you were playing the part of Saint Winifred,' he said, 'you added some words to those I prepared for you, but why? You said, "I never wanted to leave my resting-place here in Gwytherin. I sent a good man to speak for me." I didn't tell you to say those words. Where did they come from?'

She turned and looked at him, surprised. 'Did I say that? I don't remember. The words just seemed to . . . come.'

'Perhaps the saint was speaking *through* you,' said Engelard. 'These strangers had dreams and visions, and explained them to their advantage, but nobody really asked Saint Winifred what *she* wanted.'

Cadfael smiled to himself. 'How true!' he thought. 'And why not try to make everyone happy? A few hours ago, at evening prayers, Columbanus prayed loudly for Winifred to take him up out of this world. Well, he got his wish! And perhaps the saint really did speak through Sioned. Who am I to question it? Perhaps she really does want to stay in her own village. Well, her grave was opened and filled in today. No one will notice if it's opened and filled in again tonight.'

'You've had an idea,' said Sioned, watching him.

'Yes,' said Cadfael. 'Now, take that sheet and put it under the flowering trees near the gate. Shake them, and collect the petals that fall. The last time she came to him was in a cloud of white petals, so that's how she'll come this time.'

Sioned, understanding nothing yet, took the sheet and went outside.

'Give me the knife,' Cadfael said to Engelard, and he moved the light nearer to the saint's coffin. 'Thank God he didn't bleed. His habit isn't marked. Take off his clothes!'

* * *

They finished before daylight. All three of them walked down towards the village, and separated where the path turned uphill towards Rhisiart's land.

'Take Engelard home with you,' Cadfael told Sioned, 'but keep him out of sight until we're gone. And don't worry, neither the prince nor his bailiff will investigate any more. I'll speak to Peredur, he'll speak to the bailiff, and the bailiff will speak to the prince. And if the monks of Shrewsbury are happy, and the people of Gwytherin are happy (and they'll hear the news fast enough), why will anyone want to make trouble by saying what's best left unsaid?'

65

'My father can rest in peace now, thanks to you.'

'One thing I know,' said Sioned. 'My father can rest in peace now, thanks to you.' And she threw her arms around Cadfael and kissed him.

*   *   *

As Cadfael went past the river, he dropped Columbanus' knife into deep water, then walked on. 'What a good thing,' he thought, 'that the brothers who made the reliquary used a really heavy metal to make the inside walls of the box.'

8

CADFAEL PLEASES EVERYONE

I t was a bright, clear morning when everyone came out of the church after morning prayers, and took the path up to the old burial ground and the chapel. Other villagers joined the crowd on the way.

Peredur walked beside Cadfael.

'You can do something for me and for Gwytherin,' said Cadfael quietly into his ear. He went on to explain the message he wanted to get to the prince's bailiff.

'So it's like that, is it!' said Peredur when Cadfael had finished. 'And that's how you want to leave it?'

'Yes,' said Cadfael. 'It helps everyone – Saint Winifred most of all – and nobody loses anything. And it helps Sioned and Engelard, of course.' He looked hard at Peredur.

'Yes, I . . . I'm glad for them,' said Peredur bravely. 'And in a year or two, when everyone's forgotten about the deer Engelard killed, he'll be able to go back to England whenever he wants. When his father dies, he'll have land there too. Yes, I'll take your message to the bailiff today, Brother Cadfael. I'll tell him the terrible thing that I did, as well as what everyone must know but nobody must say out loud.'

'Good!' said Cadfael. 'The bailiff will do the rest. A word to the prince, and then everything will be quietly forgotten.'

They came to the path leading to Rhisiart's land, where Cai

and other servants met them. Engelard and John were not there, of course; and Sioned and Annest, on Cadfael's orders, had also stayed at home.

When they arrived at the burial ground, Prior Robert stopped at the gate. He turned to speak to the crowd.

'Father Huw, and good people of Gwytherin,' he said. 'We came here on holy business, with the blessings of your prince and bishop. If our visit has brought trouble and unhappiness to you, we are truly sorry. But now you are willing to let us take Saint Winifred's relics away with us to a greater glory, and for that we are grateful.'

Everyone seemed to be whispering their agreement with the prior's words. Then Bened stepped out of the crowd.

'Father Prior,' he said. 'We all now believe that the relics in the chapel are yours to take. All the signs have shown us that these bones rightly belong with you in Shrewsbury.'

Cadfael looked closely at all those calm, smiling, secretive faces. 'They know already!' he thought. 'They know everything! But they'll say nothing until after we're gone.'

Prior Robert walked to the chapel door, pushed it open, and stood in the doorway.

'Brother Columbanus, we are here. Your watch is over.'

He stepped inside – and stopped. The air was full of a heavy sweetness, and on the reliquary, on the prayer-desks, and all over the floor lay a soft carpet of snow-white petals. But there was nobody kneeling in prayer; only empty clothes lying on the floor.

'Columbanus . . .! He's not here!' cried the prior.

But there was nobody kneeling in prayer;
only empty clothes lying on the floor.

Brother Richard came to the prior's left shoulder, Brother Jerome to the right. Bened, Cadwallon, Cai and the others crowded in after them. Prior Robert went slowly forward to look closely at all that was left of Brother Columbanus. The black habit was lying where he had knelt, the arms out to the sides like wings.

'His shirt is still inside his habit!' whispered Brother Richard. 'And look, his shoes, they're under the edge of the habit. He's been lifted out of his clothes. It's like . . . like a snake leaving its old skin and coming out in a new . . .!'

'Oh, wonderful, truly wonderful!' said Prior Robert.

'It is a miracle!' whispered Brother Richard, in wonder.

'I remember now, the prayer he made last night,' said Prior Robert. 'He prayed aloud to the saint to take him out of this imperfect world, up into a world of holiness and light. And, surely, his prayer has been answered . . .'

'Father, shall we search? Here and in the forest?'

'Why?' said the prior. 'He wouldn't run away in the night without his clothes. No, he's gone beyond forests, and out of this world. We will say prayers for Brother Columbanus, and then we will go out and tell the world about this miracle!'

He began to pray in a loud, clear voice, with the cloud of white petals at his feet. The people of Gwytherin watched and listened, and said nothing.

'Now,' said Prior Robert, 'let us lift up this holy lady, and thank God for the heavy load.' And he moved forward to offer his own hands and shoulder.

This was Brother Cadfael's worst moment – it was the one

thing he had forgotten. But Bened was quick to save him.

'Are the people of Gwytherin only going to stand and watch, now that peace is made?' he said, and hurried forward to put his shoulder under the head end of the coffin before the prior could reach it. Six more men from the village quickly followed him. Brother Jerome was the only monk who managed to get a shoulder to it.

'Father Prior, who would believe those little bones could be so heavy?' he said, surprised.

'We are surrounded by miracles both great and small!' said Cadfael hurriedly. 'Father Prior thanked God for the load we carry. Isn't this heaviness proof of the saint's great holiness?'

'What rubbish I'm speaking!' he thought. 'But the prior will accept anything that adds to his moment of glory.'

The villagers had fetched a cart for them, and now they placed the reliquary on it for the journey to Shrewsbury.

'I'll see you in Shrewsbury one day, Cadfael,' said Bened. 'For years I've wanted to walk across England to the holy place at Walsingham. Shrewsbury would be a good place to stop and rest for a night.'

And at last, when everything was ready and Prior Robert was getting on his horse, Cai whispered in Cadfael's ear.

'When you're up on the hill where you saw us ploughing that first day, look across to the trees for a moment. We'll be there – and that's for you.'

The people of Gwytherin watched them ride away. At the top of the hill Cadfael looked across to the trees, and saw a group of people there. There was a head of black hair, with a fair head beside it. There was Cai's white bandage, and a light-brown head very close to a red one – Brother John, for sure. They were all waving and smiling, and Cadfael smiled and waved back. Then he moved on – and the trees hid them.

* * *

More than two years later, in the middle of a bright June afternoon, Brother Cadfael was coming from the abbey gardens when he saw someone arriving at the gate.

It was Bened, on his way to Walsingham.

Later, when they were sitting together in a corner of the herb garden with a bottle of wine, Bened said, 'I wanted to come before I was too old to enjoy the journey. And why not, now that I have a good young blacksmith to look after things for me? John learned quickly. Oh yes, he and Annest were married eighteen months ago, and they're very happy.'

'Do they have a child yet?' asked Cadfael.

'There's one coming soon,' said Bened. 'He'll be with us by the time I get back.'

'And Sioned and Engelard? There was no trouble after we left?' asked Cadfael.

'No, bless you! No trouble at all,' said Bened. 'They're married, and they send you their best wishes. They have a son – three months old now – and they've named him Cadfael!'

'Well, well!' said Cadfael, deeply pleased.

The next morning, Bened gave the good wishes of the people of Gwytherin to the monks of Shrewsbury. Abbot Heribert was interested to hear about the chapel and the burial ground – and the grave that had been Saint Winifred's.

'More people go there for help than ever before,' said Bened. 'And wonderful things have happened.'

Prior Robert looked surprised, then disbelieving, and as Bened went on, more and more annoyed.

'A man blind for years came, and went away seeing! A young man whose broken leg had mended badly danced by the grave. The pain went away and his bones straightened!'

'Really?' said Prior Robert, jealously. Nothing like this had happened in Shrewsbury during the last two years.

'There was a child who had a fit, and stopped breathing,' said Bened. 'His mother ran across the fields with him to Saint Winifred's grave, and put him down on the grass, dead. But immediately he began to breathe!'

'Prior Robert,' said Cadfael. 'What wonderful proof this is of Saint Winifred's great holiness! Even the grave that once held her bones works miracles! We can be proud that she rests here in our abbey, don't you agree?'

But Prior Robert was too angry to speak.

*   *   *

'Was all that true?' Cadfael asked Bened as he left.

'Yes!' said Bened. 'These things happened, and are still happening.' He smiled, and walked away down the road.

Cadfael watched him go, then turned back towards his garden. 'I think I did the best I could,' he thought happily. 'The little Welsh saint is where she wanted to be, and is looking after her own people. She won't mind lying on top of Rhisiart's bones! And we've got what belonged to us in the first place. What could be better than that?'

GLOSSARY

abbey a church with buildings where monks live
alibi proof that you were somewhere else when a crime happened
arrow a long thin piece of wood with a point at one end
bailiff an officer of the law who works for a king or prince
bandage a piece of cloth tied round a part of the body that is hurt
Benedictine following the way of life taught by St Benedict
bishop an important priest in the Christian Church
blacksmith someone who makes or mends things made of iron
bless to ask for God's help for somebody or something
bow a curved piece of wood with a string joining the ends;
    a weapon used for shooting arrows
cart a vehicle for carrying things, pulled by a horse
chapel a small church
coffin a box in which a dead body is buried
coward a person who is not brave in dangerous or difficult times
cross *(n)* something with this shape +, often used as the sign of
    the Christian Church
curse *(n)* words that can make something bad happen to someone
deer a wild animal that eats grass and can run fast
determined very certain that you want to do something
devil an evil spirit
Father when you speak to a priest, you call him 'Father'
feather feathers are the soft light things that cover a bird's body
fit *(n)* a sudden illness, where a person is unconscious for a time
forgive to stop being angry with someone for a bad thing they did
glory fame, praise, and respect (for doing great things)
grave *(n)* a hole in the ground where a dead person is buried
habit the special clothes that a monk wears

herb a plant used to make medicines or to make food taste good

herbalist a person who uses herbs for medicines

holy connected with God or a religion; the Holy Land means the parts of Israel and Palestine that are important to Christianity

jug a large pot with a handle, used to hold water, beer, etc.

load *(n)* something that is carried (by a person, horse, etc.)

loft the room or space under the roof of a house

messenger a person who carries a message

miracle a wonderful and surprising thing that happens, but which cannot be explained by the laws of nature

monastery the buildings where monks live, work, and pray

monk (also called **brother**) a man who gives his life to God, living and working in a monastery

motive a reason for doing something (especially a crime)

niece the daughter of your brother or sister

ox (plural **oxen**) a male cow, used for heavy work on a farm

petal one of the coloured parts of a flower

ploughman a man who guides animals to pull a plough (a machine for digging the land)

pray (*noun* **prayer**) to send a message, silent or spoken, to God

priest an official of the Christian Church

prince the son of a king

relics parts of the body or clothes of a holy person who has died

reliquary a special kind of box or coffin in which relics are kept

saint a person that the Christian Church recognizes as very holy, because of the way they lived or died

sword a weapon with a long sharp piece of metal and a handle

vision a kind of dream about holy things or people

well *(n)* a deep hole for getting water from under the ground

Before Reading

1 **Read the story introduction on the first page of the book, and the back cover. Are these sentences true (T) or false (F)?**

1 The people of Gwytherin are happy for Saint Winifred's bones to go to England. T/F
2 The person who dies in this story is shot with a gun. T/F
3 Brother Cadfael is a detective as well as a monk and a gardener. T/F
4 The murder happens in a village in Wales. T/F

2 **One of these people is the murderer – and one is the person who is murdered. Can you guess who they are?**

1 a monk
2 an English farm worker
3 a young Welshman
4 A Welsh land-owner
5 A beautiful Welsh girl
6 An officer of the king

3 **What do you think happens to the 'bones' of the title? You can choose more than one idea.**

They are . . .
1 found, then lost again.
2 taken to England.
3 kept in a holy place.
4 dry and powdery, and soon turn to dust.
5 dug up, then buried again.
6 used for making medicine.
7 thrown into the sea.
8 used for making music.

While Reading

Read Chapters 1 to 3. Choose the best question-word for these questions, and then answer them.

What / Why

1 . . . did Cadfael do before he became a monk?
2 . . . did Winifred tell Brother Jerome in his dream?
3 . . . did Cadfael want Brother John to go to Wales?
4 . . . didn't Rhisiart want his daughter to marry Engelard?
5 . . . was Prior Robert's big mistake?
6 . . . did Rhisiart expect very little from a second meeting?

Before you read Chapter 4, can you guess who killed Rhisiart? Match each person with a possible motive from the list, and then write P (Perhaps) or N (No) by each name.

Sioned   Prior Robert   Brother Jerome
Engelard   Father Huw   Brother Columbanus

Possible motives for killing Rhisiart:

1 Because he desperately wanted to take the saint's relics back to Shrewsbury for his own glory.
2 Because he had had a vision telling him to do it.
3 Because Rhisiart wouldn't let him marry Sioned.
4 Because Prior Robert had ordered him to do it.
5 Because Rhisiart wouldn't let her marry Engelard.
6 Because he wanted the monks to take the relics and leave.

Read Chapter 4. Then put these sentences into the right order to show what Cadfael knows about Rhisiart's death.

1 Someone pushed an arrow into Rhisiart's chest.
2 Someone put a knife in his back and killed him.
3 There was a short sharp shower of rain.
4 Some hours later, Bened found Rhisiart's body.
5 Rhisiart left the fields and walked through the forest towards Father Huw's house.
6 Someone turned Rhisiart's body onto his back.
7 He fell onto his face on the grass.

Read Chapter 5. Who said this, and to whom? Who, or what, are they talking about?

1 'Is that too much to ask?'
2 'You may do what she asks.'
3 'He's not dead, nor is he in any danger.'
4 'These are great wonders indeed!'
5 'He cannot accuse me!'
6 'Did *you* believe it?'
7 'I still want you to do it.'

Before you read Chapter 6, *The bottle of poppy medicine*, what do you think the medicine has been used for?

1 to make someone well
2 to kill someone
3 to make someone sleep
4 to make someone tell the truth

Read Chapters 6 and 7, then match these halves of sentences.

1 When Cadfael saw how much poppy medicine had gone,

2 Annest asked if it was wrong for Brother John to love her,

3 Cai helped Brother John get away from Rhisiart's house

4 Sioned acted the part of Saint Winifred in the chapel,

5 Engelard was so angry when he saw Sioned's wounded arm

6 Cadfael knew that it was no good telling the truth

7 . . . before the bailiff arrived to take him away.

8 . . . he wondered what Columbanus had used it for.

9 . . . because nobody would believe that Columbanus was a murderer.

10 . . . which frightened Columbanus into telling the truth about Rhisiart's murder.

11 . . . but Cadfael told her that everyone should be allowed one new beginning.

12 . . . that he lifted Columbanus and shook him violently.

Before you read Chapter 8, can you guess the answers to these questions? Choose from these names.

Bened / Brother Cadfael / Brother Colombanus / Engelard / Peredur / Saint Winifred

1 Who will stay in Gwytherin – in a grave?

2 Who will travel to Shrewsbury in the reliquary?

3 Who will marry Sioned?

4 Who will visit Cadfael with news from Gwytherin?

5 Who will have the same name as a new baby in Gwytherin?

After Reading

1 **Perhaps this is what some of the characters in the story were thinking. Which characters are they, and what is happening in the story at this moment? Then put the passages in the right order for the story.**

   1 'He's a good, kind man. He said he'd come today, as soon as he could, so I will sit here quietly by my father and wait for him. I have kept the clothes, as he asked – he seems to think they will tell him something. I hope so.'

   2 'Right – off to the forest! Cai's told me a good place to go, where the bailiff will never find me. I know I'm doing the right thing. My life is here, with Annest, not in the abbey.'

   3 'I wish those two weren't coming to Wales with us. The boy's not suitable at all, and as for Cadfael – he's always asleep when I talk about holy relics in our meetings!'

   4 'What's going on? What are all these people doing here? And there's Sioned – she looks ill! Why is she staring at me like that? I must go to her. What . . . Oh no, oh no!'

   5 'What's he talking about? What does he mean – it's mine? He's surely not . . . oh yes, he is! The bag must be full of gold. It's a bribe! I don't believe it – does this stupid man really think he can *buy* our saint?'

2 What exactly did Cadfael, Sioned, and Engelard do before they left the chapel on the night that Brother Columbanus died? Use these notes to write a short description.

- Columbanus's habit, shirt, and shoes
- reliquary, saint's bones, Columbanus's dead body
- saint's grave, saint's bones, Rhisiart's body
- white petals from the flowers on the trees

3 On his last day in Gwytherin Cadfael asks Peredur to take a message to the prince's bailiff. What does he say? Complete Cadfael's part of the conversation in your own words.

PEREDUR: Of course I'll take your message, Brother Cadfael. What is it? Is it about the murder?

CADFAEL: _____

PEREDUR: I never thought he was. So who did do it?

CADFAEL: _____

PEREDUR: One of the—! Oh, that's terrible! And you say he died last night at the chapel? How did that happen?

CADFAEL: _____

PEREDUR: Yes, he would be very angry if anyone tried to harm Sioned. And he's very strong. So where is the body?

CADFAEL: _____

PEREDUR: What?! You're taking – but where are the relics?

CADFAEL: _____

PEREDUR: I wasn't shouting. But does Prior Robert know?

CADFAEL: _____

PEREDUR: Yes, I suppose that is the best thing for everyone.

4 The day after the murder Sioned goes to find Engelard in his
hiding-place, to tell him what has been happening. Use the
linking words below to complete what she says.

*and / anyway / because / because / before / but / but / since /
so / that / that / what / when / while / who*

'Let me tell you _____'s been happening. _____ I arrived at
the church yesterday evening, I expected to see my father
there, _____ nobody had seen him _____ he left the house
with you in the morning. We were all worried, _____ Father
Huw said evening prayers must wait _____ we looked for
him. It was Bened _____ found him. Prior Robert said it was
Saint's Winifred's revenge, _____ when Bened recognized
your arrow, people began to say _____ you and my father had
often argued about me. _____, you know what happened next
_____ you arrived about then. But listen, Brother Cadfael is
helping me, _____ we've found out _____ your arrow did not
kill my father _____ he was already dead – killed by a knife in
his back _____ your arrow was pushed into his chest!'

5 Here are some different ways for the story to end. Choose the
ending you like best, and complete it. Use as many words as you
like.

1 Peredur saw the accident when Colombanus died. The next
day, he told . . .

2 Engelard caught Brother Colombanus, and they tied his
arms behind his back and took him down to Prior Robert.
But Columbanus said . . .

3 Engelard did not catch Brother Colombanus, who disappeared into the night. The next day . . .

4 After Bened's news from Gwytherin, Prior Robert asked for the reliquary to be opened. He found . . .

6 Here are some different titles for this story. Which ones do you prefer, and why? Are there any which are not suitable?

The Box of Bones	Cadfael's First Case
Saint Winifred's Revenge	A Holy Death
Murder in Gwytherin	The White Petals of Death
Rhisiart and the Relics	Murder and Miracles
The Arrow of Death	Murder Comes with the English

7 What kind of person makes a good detective? Look at this list and give Cadfael a mark out of 10 for each one.

____ a good listener	____ understands people
____ intelligent	____ able to think quickly
____ likeable and friendly	____ able to lie easily
____ notices small details	____ willing to take risks

Now choose one thing that modern detectives have – e.g. video cameras, computers, telephones, fingerprint tests – that would be useful for Cadfael. Imagine that he had this thing in Gwytherin. How would it help him?

ABOUT THE AUTHOR

Ellis Peters is the pen name of Edith Mary Pargeter, who was born in Shropshire in 1913. She began work as a chemist's assistant and wrote novels in her spare time. Her first novel was published in 1936, and she continued to write for almost fifty years after that. Her work included modern detective novels and historical novels, but she is best known for the Brother Cadfael novels. *A Morbid Taste for Bones* (1977) was the first of these, and she went on to write another nineteen international bestsellers about the monk detective. The last one, *Brother Cadfael's Penance*, was published in 1994. More than half of the stories have been filmed for television, with the well-known actor Derek Jacobi playing Brother Cadfael.

Ellis Peters took great care to make each story a good novel with real characters, not just a mystery with an answer. She received many awards, including the Diamond Dagger of the British Crime Writers Association, and the Edgar award from the Mystery Writers of America. She died in 1995, aged 82.

After so many centuries, it is hard to know how much of Saint Winifred's story is true. However, it is known that her relics *were* taken from Gwytherin to Shrewsbury in 1138, and that people reported miracles in both places. Ellis Peters took Saint Winifred's story, her own love of Shrewsbury and Shropshire, and her knowledge of life in the middle ages – and Brother Cadfael appeared. The books are so popular that thousands of people go to Shrewsbury every year to go on a 'Cadfael tour', visiting places that appear in the books.

ABOUT BOOKWORMS

OXFORD BOOKWORMS LIBRARY

*Classics • True Stories • Fantasy & Horror • Human Interest
Crime & Mystery • Thriller & Adventure*

The OXFORD BOOKWORMS LIBRARY offers a wide range of original and adapted stories, both classic and modern, which take learners from elementary to advanced level through six carefully graded language stages:

Stage 1 (400 headwords)	**Stage 4** (1400 headwords)
Stage 2 (700 headwords)	**Stage 5** (1800 headwords)
Stage 3 (1000 headwords)	**Stage 6** (2500 headwords)

More than fifty titles are also available on cassette, and there are many titles at Stages 1 to 4 which are specially recommended for younger learners. In addition to the introductions and activities in each Bookworm, resource material includes photocopiable test worksheets and Teacher's Handbooks, which contain advice on running a class library and using cassettes, and the answers for the activities in the books.

Several other series are linked to the OXFORD BOOKWORMS LIBRARY. They range from highly illustrated readers for young learners, to playscripts, non-fiction readers, and unsimplified texts for advanced learners.

Oxford Bookworms Starters	*Oxford Bookworms Factfiles*
Oxford Bookworms Playscripts	*Oxford Bookworms Collection*

Details of these series and a full list of all titles in the OXFORD BOOKWORMS LIBRARY can be found in the *Oxford English* catalogues. A selection of titles from the OXFORD BOOKWORMS LIBRARY can be found on the next pages.

The Big Sleep

RAYMOND CHANDLER

Retold by Rosalie Kerr

General Sternwood has four million dollars, and two young daughters, both pretty and both wild. He's an old, sick man, close to death, but he doesn't like being blackmailed. So he asks private detective Philip Marlowe to get the blackmailer off his back.

Marlowe knows the dark side of life in Los Angeles well, and nothing much surprises him. But the Sternwood girls are a lot wilder than their old father realizes. They like men, drink, drugs – and it's not just a question of blackmail.

Death of an Englishman

MAGDALEN NABB

Retold by Diane Mowat

It was a very inconvenient time for murder. Florence was full of Christmas shoppers and half the police force was already on holiday.

At first it seemed quite an ordinary murder. Of course, there are always a few mysteries. In this case, the dead man had been in the habit of moving his furniture at three o'clock in the morning. Naturally, the police wanted to know why. The case became more complicated. But all the time, the answer was right under their noses. They just couldn't see it. It was, after all, a very ordinary murder.

The Eagle of the Ninth

ROSEMARY SUTCLIFF

Retold by John Escott

In the second century AD, when the Ninth Roman Legion marched into the mists of northern Britain, not one man came back. Four thousand men disappeared, and the Eagle, the symbol of the Legion's honour, was lost.

Years later there is a story that the Eagle has been seen again. So Marcus Aquila, whose father disappeared with the Ninth, travels north, to find the Eagle and bring it back, and to learn how his father died. But the tribes of the north are wild and dangerous, and they hate the Romans . . .

The Hound of the Baskervilles

SIR ARTHUR CONAN DOYLE

Retold by Patrick Nobes

Dartmoor. A wild, wet place in the south-west of England. A place where it is easy to get lost, and to fall into the soft green earth which can pull the strongest man down to his death.

A man is running for his life. Behind him comes an enormous dog – a dog from his worst dreams, a dog from hell. Between him and a terrible death stands only one person – the greatest detective of all time, Sherlock Holmes.

BOOKWORMS · CLASSICS · STAGE 4

The Scarlet Letter

NATHANIEL HAWTHORNE

Retold by John Escott

Scarlet is the colour of sin, and the letter 'A' stands for 'Adultery'. In the 1600s, in Boston, Massachusetts, love was allowed only between a husband and a wife. A child born outside marriage was a child of sin.

Hester Prynne must wear the scarlet letter on her dress for the rest of her life. How can she ever escape from this public shame? What will happen to her child, growing up in the shadow of the scarlet letter? The future holds no joy for Hester Prynne.

And what will happen to her sinful lover – the father of her child?

BOOKWORMS · CRIME & MYSTERY · STAGE 5

The Dead of Jericho

COLIN DEXTER

Retold by Clare West

Chief Inspector Morse is drinking a pint of beer. He is thinking about an attractive woman who lives not far away.

The woman he is thinking of is hanging, dead, from the ceiling of her kitchen. On the floor lies a chair, almost two metres away from the woman's feet.

Chief Inspector Morse finishes his pint, and orders another. Perhaps he will visit Anne, after all. But he is in no particular hurry. Meanwhile, Anne is still hanging in her kitchen, waiting for the police to come and cut her down. She is in no hurry, either.